Balancing & Sport Acrobatics

Stan Buchholtz

ARCO PUBLISHING COMPANY, INC.
NEW YORK

Published by Arco Publishing Company, Inc.
219 Park Avenue South, New York, N.Y. 10003

Library of Congress Cataloging in Publication Data

Buchholtz, Stan.
  Balancing and sport acrobatics.

  Includes index.
  1. Acrobats and acrobatism. I. Title.
GV551.B8   796.4'7   77-14388
ISBN 0-668-04396-2

Printed in the United States of America

Acknowledgment

I wish to thank the Mystic Community Center and its director, Roger Quesnel, for the use of the facilities and for making this book possible. Much appreciated is the enthusiasm of my models Bob Carver, coach Nicky Checker, John Foley, Lynn Heffernan, Paul Humphreys, and Jack Morehouse.

My very special thanks to my patient balancing partners Rhonda McCabe, Suzanne Meader, and Anna Sullivan, and to Steve Schumaker for his able assistance.

Preface

Although balancing and acrobatics have long been popular forms of recreation, they have tended to be restricted to a relatively small group of athletes and professional performers. The Olympic games of recent years have created a tremendous public interest in gymnastics in general, and figures such as Kathy Rigby, Olga Korbut, and Nadia Comaneci, with their incredibly impressive abilities, have done much to open new horizons to girls in particular.

Sport acrobatics, however, is now emerging as a separate entity, with international competition exclusive of the formal gymnastic disciplines. Because of its versatility, it is well suited to both boys and girls, and men and women of all ages. It can be performed alone or in groups, with only moderate skill and strength to begin with, and can progress as far as imagination, energy, and enthusiasm will permit. Little or no equipment is mandatory, and a backyard lawn provides as much opportunity as the most sophisticated gymnasium, where, it may be added, only a mat is required.

The scope of this book is to provide a reference text in the art of balancing and sport acrobatics for the beginner as well as the more advanced participant, emphasizing those helpful pointers that are so often overlooked in textbooks of this nature. It hopes to supply a system of progression from the very elementary to the more difficult stunts, and to offer suggestions for and examples of combinations which can tie together into smoothly and kinesthetically pleasing routines all of the individual skills the students have mastered.

The rewards are, of course, the satisfaction of accomplishment, improvement in strength and all-around body condition, and, most of all, just plain fun!

Stan Buchholtz
Mystic, 1978

List of Illustrations

Contents

Introduction

Just as it is usually more advisable to begin building a house with the foundation and work upwards, it is best to begin balancing and acrobatics with the more elementary moves in order to provide a solid foundation of skills and strength. Many beginners are so impressed with the spectacular stunts of advanced performers who "make it all look so easy," that they attempt moves which put them into positions they are not qualified to recover from. The injuries that may be sustained under such conditions often discourage further efforts and, at the very least, inhibit the learning process. Safety should always be an important part of any training program, and discipline really need in no way impair the enjoyment of the sport.

When working alone, always plan your moves so that you are familiar with a variety of safe recovery methods. Whenever possible, spotters should be used. By discussing moves in advance, performers and spotters become thoroughly familiar with the attempted stunts. A good spotter provides one of the most valuable aids in building the confidence that is so necessary during the learning process, and he should be on the alert to offer constructive suggestions.

RECOVERY TECHNIQUES

The danger of injury resulting from most falls can be considerably reduced or eliminated altogether by the use of a few elementary principles and techniques.

1. *Increasing the distance through which the impact of the fall is dissipated.* For example, when landing on the feet, let the balls of the feet make contact before the heels, and bend the knees to absorb the shock.

2. *Increase the area of contact.* Rather than falling on a hand or elbow, try to distribute the impact over the entire arm and side of the body. Karate practitioners spend considerable time in developing a rather noisy but effective method of slapping the mat and exhaling loudly upon ground contact after a throw.

I Forward Roll

II

III

3. *Forward roll.* Rolling represents a very advantageous method of recovery from certain falls by transforming lateral motion into rotary motion. The beginner should start from a squatting position, with hands placed at about shoulder width on the ground (I). Duck the head under, and push off with the legs to start the roll (II). Although the head may touch the ground, the weight should be carried by the arms as long as possible, until the upper back and shoulders make contact. The body must remain tightly tucked until the feet once again touch, and the arms are thrown forward to grasp the shins (III). When properly done, there should be enough momentum to permit rising to the standing position without losing balance backwards. The move must be done smoothly and quickly, and not result in any jolting to the head.

Advanced performers learn to start the roll from the standing position, or even with a run and diving motion. This requires more arm strength, but results in acquisition of greater self-confidence and recovery skill.

IV Backward Roll

V

VI

4. *Backward roll.* Assume the same initial position as for the forward roll (IV), rock forward slightly, and then push off backwards briskly. As soon as the hands leave the ground, rotate the arms backwards while rolling on the seat and back, and keep the knees and chin firmly tucked. Place the hands above the shoulders with the fingers pointing in the line of the roll (V), and roll over onto the feet (VI).

This move is more difficult than the forward roll, and the tendency is to fall off to either side when rolling over the head. The initial push-off should be quite vigorous in order to acquire sufficient rolling momentum to complete the move.

VII Shoulder Roll

VIII

IX

5. *Shoulder roll.* This method may be executed when the performer is not facing in such a way as to roll either forward or backwards. Stand at an angle to the direction of travel, feet spread moderately, lean forward and to the side with the leading arm forming an arc downwards (VII). Try to contact the ground with the back of the upper arm and continue rolling on the shoulder and back (VIII). The momentum should be sufficient to bring the performer back onto the feet (IX). After some practice, this stunt may be attempted from a run, simulating an unanticipated fall.

ATTITUDE

Mental outlook is probably the single most important element in any undertaking, and notably so in sports. The value of competition in character building has often been overrated and much abused. Striving for excellence should really be a matter of personal pride. Emphasis on sincere mutual recognition and encouragement, combined with the appreciation of each participant's individuality, can do more for the advancement of skills and pure enjoyment than the constant struggle to perform better than someone else. Physical activity should be an integral part of everyone's lifestyle. We engage in sports in order to maintain and improve our mental and physical health, and unnecessary mental pressures more often than not have negative results.

PREPARATION AND WARM-UP

Although strength is always an advantage in acrobatics, the required degree can gradually be attained over a period of time. For the more serious performer, the concurrent use of gymnastic apparatus and weight training will be very helpful.

Before each workout session, a period of calisthenics and stretching exercises is highly recommended. All muscles should be moved through a complete range of extensions and contractions in order to be thoroughly warmed up and prepared. Such exercises as jumping jacks, toe touches, arm circles, sit-ups, leg raises, push-ups, and trunk twisting are but a few excellent examples. Sufficient repetitions should be used to work up a mild sweat and stimulate curculation, but without stressing muscles to the point of tiring. Additional strength-building exercises can always be performed at the end of a session, when the acrobatic practice has been completed.

In the beginning, workout sessions should be short, and then gradually extended as strength and endurance increase. Ideally, it would be best to be able to devote a part of each day to some form of exercise, but this may be difficult to arrange in light of the busy schedules many of us maintain. For most people, three times a week is more practical, and every effort should be made to be faithful to a program of this frequency.

BASIC POSITIONS

The following illustrations will clarify and define some of the terminology used in this text.

These positions refer to the relationship of various parts of the body to each other, irrespective of the attitude towards the ground.

Fig. X Straight or extended

Fig. XI Arch

Fig. XII Tuck

Fig. XIII Pike

Fig. XIV Half lever, or "L"

Fig. XV Straddle

Fig. XVI Split

Fig. XVII Stag

Fig. XVIII Scale

Fig. XIX Frontal balance

FORM

It may be asking too much in the beginning to expect perfect form—such as always keeping toes pointed, etc.—but it is nevertheless advisable to stress the value of proper technique from the start. Pointing toes, keeping legs straight and together where required, and generally maintaining a firm and erect posture not only contribute vastly to the pleasing appearance of acrobatic moves, but facilitate their performance. Any learning process may be shortened by eliminating as many of the variables as possible. When attempting a hand balance, for example, if the legs and hips are kept rigid automatically, learning to control movement is reduced to the use of the shoulders, arms, and hands. If the body is kept in a rather limp attitude, there are just too many shifting weight centers for the beginner to think about, and the results are erratic.

PART I

Singles Balancing

DIFFICULTY NOTATION

As far as possible, the sequence of the skills described will be in their order of difficulty. In addition, a notation of stars, from one (*), for the simplest, to five (*****), for the most difficult, will be used.

LINE OF BALANCE

We hardly consider simply standing on our feet or walking a great accomplishment, until we watch a young child in the process of learning these basics. There are actually many skills involved which we take entirely for granted, and an analysis of the mechanics involved will be very helpful to us in understanding the problems of balancing on our heads or hands. In physics, the weight of any body is considered, for analytical purposes, to be concentrated at one point called the center of gravity (c.g.). If we draw a line vertically through the base—the base being either hand, the feet, or the head—then the c.g. will lie on this line when the body is in a balanced, static position.

If one thinks of this in more lifelike terms, equal portions of the body must be distributed on either side of the line of balance. If the weight shifts to any one side, equilibrium no longer exists, and a corrective force must be applied or the body will fall in the direction of the imbalance. The beginner generally tends to overcorrect, or apply corrective action too late, thus making control erratic. It is important to have a clear mental image of the balance position, and be aware of how various body movements affect that position.

Each person's body structure differs from that of another so that, although the principles are common to all, special consideration must be given to these individual differences. Some skills will be more easily learned by one person, while that person may have trouble accomplishing what seems easy to others. Such inconsistencies may be the result of physical differences rather than simply variations in motor skills.

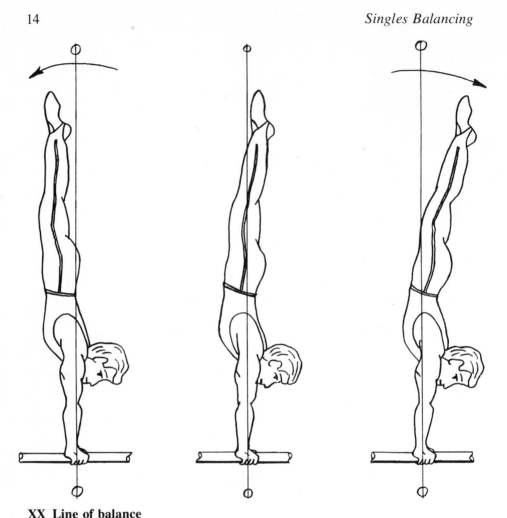

XX Line of balance

BALANCES

1. Head balance*

This stunt forms the basic building block for many balancing skills. Mastery of it and its variations will be most helpful in establishing the pattern for more advanced work.

Tuck press

Begin by assuming the squat position, as in a forward roll. Place the head on the ground so that the hands and head form a tripod base, using the forward

1a Head balance tuck press

1b

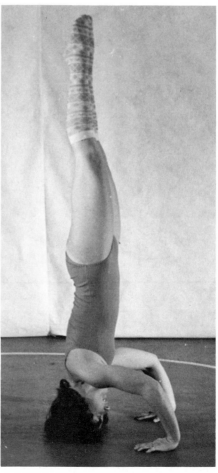

1c

part of the head rather than the very top or back. Now raise the hips to a position over the head by extending the legs (a). Keep the thighs close to the chest, and press down firmly with the hands. As the feet lift off the floor, rotate from the hips, keeping a tightly tucked position (b). When the legs are well overhead, slowly extend them until they are straight (c). To come down from the balance, reverse the process, and return the feet to the starting position slowly. In case of an overbalance, tuck briskly into a forward roll. Do not fall over in the extended position!

Pointers: About ⅔ of the weight is borne by the head, the hands applying the balancing force. Do not shoot the legs upward rapidly to "catch" the balance. Control must be sure at every step of the way. Assume a straight or slightly arched final position with back, buttocks, and leg muscles firm. Toes should be pointed, as in all balances, to aid in control. Be aware of the location of the hips throughout the move.

Kick-up

With the hands and head in position, extend either leg. Push off with the bent leg and throw the extended leg upward smoothly (d). The straight leg will reach the final position first, with the other leg rising and extending to join it.

Pointers: Start with a gentle kick to acquire the feel, and gradually kick harder with each successive attempt. When returning the feet to the floor, keep the hips on the line of balance as long as possible to slow the descent, which should be as smooth and controlled as the kick-up.

Straddle press

Place the hands and head in the tripod base position and extend both legs to a straddle. Bend sharply at the waist, as the hips will have to be brought well past the line of balance to permit the legs to lift off the ground (e). Keep the legs straight, but bring them together as they approach the vertical. It is important to allow the hips to return gradually to the line of balance as the legs rise, in order to avoid overbalancing. Reverse the procedure to come down again.

Pointers: An excellent exercise consists of bringing the straddled legs down as far as possible without touching the floor, and then returning to the balance. Properly done, this exercise will emphasize the compensating movement between legs and hips about the balance line.

1d Head balance kick-up

**1e Head balance
straddle press**

1f Head balance pike press

Pike press

This move is performed in a manner similar to the straddle press, except the legs are kept together throughout. Since the feet will be further from the line of balance at the start, it will require the hips to be brought even further past the vertical line initially (f). As before, practice controlled repetitions of this press.

Back extension

Begin by performing a backward roll, but instead of ending with the feet on the mat, extend the legs upward smartly and slide the hands to a good tripod position as the balance is approached. After mastering this technique, the extension should be learned with a pike position instead of the tuck. Sit on the mat with legs extended (g), and roll backwards with the back rounded as much as possible to give smoothness to the move (h). Follow through as before, but keep the legs extended throughout (i).

1g Back extension to a head balance

1h

1i

2a Head and forearm balance   **3a Forearm balance**

2. Head and forearm balance*

Clasp the hands on top of the head and place forearms and head on the mat in a good tripod base. The fingers should be on the mat in such a position as to avoid getting pinched under the head. Kick or press up to the balance using the elbows for control (a).

3. Forearm balance (Tiger stand)**

Place the forearms on the floor nearly parallel to each other, with the hands spread flat and the upper arms as close to vertical as possible. Eyes should be directed at a point midway between the thumbs. Kick up into a fairly straight position. Rotate and stretch strongly from the shoulders (a). The tendency to sag down and forward must be firmly resisted.

This position may also be entered from the head and forearm balance by lifting the head, sliding the hands flat, and stretching up.

A short combination of moves consists of a head balance first, then moving the arms one at a time to the head and forearm position, and finally lifting the head to obtain a tiger stand.

4. Hand balance***

This stunt requires a great deal of practice to perfect, but offers endless variety and much satisfaction. It may be performed alone or with partners, on the floor, mat, or on apparatus. It will be very helpful for the performer to construct a set of small portable parallel or ground bars. The author still has in his possession, and still uses, a pair he built some thirty years ago. Common building lumber may be used. The bars can be about 24" long, and the crosspieces 12" each. Consider the dimensions given as a rough guide. The important thing is that the diameter of the bars be large enough to afford a comfortable grip.

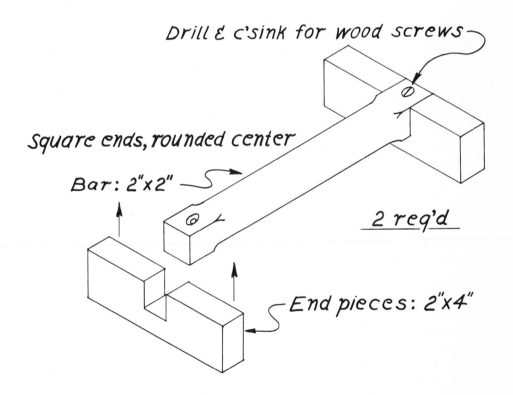

4a Ground parallel bars

Preparation for hand balancing: Exercise the wrists prior to each balancing session by repeatedly pushing each hand with the other over and back as far as it will go.

4b Kick-up to hand balance   **4c**

Kick-up

There are several stages involved in mastering the hand balance. When not using the bars, place the hands on the floor about shoulder width apart, index fingers pointing straight ahead, with the rest of the fingers spread outwards. The fingers should support about one-third of the body weight, the remainder being borne by the palms. Let the head hang comfortably and choose a visual reference point somewhere in a line between the finger tips. Bring either foot in towards the hands to a position which will permit a strong kick-up. If the foot is in too close, it will tend to impede the power of the kick. Too far away will result in the upper back being in an almost horizontal position. The hips should be held high, with the back closer to the final position. This will permit a much more controlled kick-up with very little back movement. After all, although the upper back must move to enter the balance posture, excessive movement is hard to stop. The other leg is left extended (b).

The first stage now consists of learning to kick up to the balance position consistently. Kicking up is best done gradually. Be patient, and do not attempt to rush this phase. Control and awareness of body position is the essence of the art. Lean forward slightly so that the shoulders are somewhat ahead of the hands. Push off gently with the bent leg and at the same time throw the straight leg upwards. The force should be only sufficient to carry the legs a short distance. The essential thing at this point is to gain a feel of how much kick is required to put the hips into the correct position. Kick a little harder each successive time and try to return the feet to the starting point slowly by keeping the upper back high and in close to the line of balance. As the balance line is approached, the shoulders must pull back slightly to a location directly over the hands, and the kicking leg joins the straight leg as described in the kick-up to a head balance (c).

Should an overbalance occur, the best recovery is to execute a quarter turn with the body and land on the feet. This method requires the least time and effort, although other techniques may be used once more proficiency is gained.

After the kick-up procedure has been established, the next stage, which is that of learning to control the balance, can be begun. When working alone, a wall may be used to help maintain the proper position. The hands are placed just far enough away from the wall to put the body into a very slight overbalance. Kick up and permit the feet to contact the wall. The beginner can now experiment with the use of the hands in controlling the balance, and must learn the proper posture.

In recent years, much study has been made of the technical side of gymnastics, and many important improvements and refinements in technique have been made possible. The author has come to certain conclusions concerning the pros and cons of old and new methods, and as is usually the case, has found a blending of ideas to be the most practical.

For the greatest amount of skeletal support, and hence the most endurance, a nearly straight posture (c) has been found to be superior to the well arched back (d). Practice stretching as high as possible from the shoulders on up. Press legs firmly together and tighten buttocks, but do not permit them to protrude as in a pike (e). Push off the wall gently with one foot while pressing down strongly with the fingers. This finger pressure is the principal means of resisting overbalance. An underbalance can be overcome by bending the arms slightly and, keeping the forearms perpendicular to the floor, thus shifting the weight back to the other side of the line of balance.

Another method of learning this phase is to work with a partner, who can grasp the legs upon kick-up and hold the balancer in the correct position to gain the feel of controlling the balance. The ground bars should also be used alternately during all stages of learning. Kick-up will have to be a bit harder

4d Excessively arched hand balance   4e Excessively straight hand balance

since the hands are somewhat higher off the ground, and the bars should be gripped tightly. The wrists provide the means of control here, and although an overbalance cannot be so strongly resisted as with the flat hand on the mat, an underbalance is much more easily controlled. In the case of an overbalance which cannot be reversed by wrist or hand action alone, it sometimes helps to permit the legs to bend quickly, causing a momentary weight shift. Control may also be regained by taking a small step forward with one or both hands alternately, although the beginner should avoid getting into the habit of regularly moving the hands to hold the balance.

On an average, it will take six to eight weeks of steady work to master the hand balance. Progress often comes in spurts, but once the position can be held for 10 to 15 seconds, it becomes more a matter of stamina and endurance. The performer can be well satisfied if the balance can be held for a period of one minute.

Walking

Once the balance has been mastered, walking on the hands can be learned. Overbalance slightly and move the hands a few inches at a time by alternately shifting the body weight from hand to hand. It may help to maintain this overbalance by turning the fingers outward somewhat. Group walking contests are usually a great source of entertainment. Practice walking in circles as well as in straight lines.

Additional Balancing Challenges

The ground bars provide the means for attempting many variations in balancing skills.

4f Wide grip hand balance

Wide grip balance

Place the bars wide apart before kicking up, or move them to each side alternately while in a hand balance (f). Avoid letting the bars slide outwards with the resultant face-to-mat collision.

4g One bar hand balance
   (overhand grip)

4h One bar hand balance
   (underhand grip)

One bar balance

Turn one bar at a right angle to the kick-up line, and use a shoulder width overhand grip (g). Also do this with a reverse, or underhand, grip (h).

4i One bar close grip hand balance   **4j One bar close grip hand balance variation**

One bar close grip balance

Try the same overhand position as previously described, but with both hands very close together (i).

A difficult variation consists of having the bar parallel to the kick-up line, with one hand directly in front of the other (j).

4k Pirouettes

Pirouettes

Grip the bars at the near end and kick up (k). Shift the weight and the balance line over to the right hand and begin pivoting to the right around the arm. The feet precede the shoulders in a slight overbalance, and the left hand pushes off and regrasps the right bar in an overhand grip (l). The weight is now shifted onto the left arm while the right hand pushes off to continue the turn, and regrasps the left bar (m). The performer has now rotated 180° and is facing in the opposite direction from his kick-up position. The body must be kept rigid throughout the move, and once again, awareness of hip position is

4l   4m

most critical. As an aid to stabilizing the first half of the turn, place the bars parallel to and at an appropriate distance from a wall so that the feet will make contact as the one bar balance position is entered.

The turns may be practiced in either direction, although it is generally easier for right-handed balancers to turn in a clockwise direction. Pirouettes are also performed in a reverse manner, turning counter-clockwise into an underhand grip on the right bar at the midpoint. They are done either quickly, without coming to a complete still balance at the midpoint, or slowly, with a momentary stop at the 90° mark. Pirouettes should also be practiced on the floor while either standing or walking on the hands.

4n Back extension to a hand balance

4o

4p

Back extension

Use the same technique as described on page 18 in the back extension to the head balance, except that the extension itself must be much more forceful in order to reduce the strength required to straighten the arms (n,o,p).

5a One arm hand balance

5. One arm hand balance*****

The aristocrat of hand balances, and the goal of all serious performers, may take years of work to perfect. Since more moves are initiated to the right, with the right arm and shoulder receiving a greater share of the workout effort, it may be worthwhile to learn the one arm balance on the left arm. This suggestion is purely a matter of personal preference.

The balance is more easily learned with the legs held in a straddle. Shift the body directly over one arm, and tilt the hips in the same direction. Stretch all the way out, especially from the shoulder, retaining the grasp on the other bar with the thumb and fingertips of the unburdened hand. Bring the head in close to the shoulder, sighting down the arm. In this position, the control of the balance is shifted gradually more and more to the supporting wrist as the other hand slowly releases its grip. Remove all but the forefinger from the bar, and reduce the weight on it to the point where it is barely touching (a).

5b

Impatience probably does more to impede progress at this stage than any other factor. Attempting to rush the process by quickly lifting the free arm only results in a sudden weight shift which is beyond the control capabilities of the single supporting wrist or hand. Many, many hours of patient practice are required with just the fingertip contact of the free hand before the controlling arm's reflexes are quick and powerful enough to resist the forces of over and underbalance, as well as the twisting tendencies.

When the point has been reached where the guiding finger is lifted, the arm should be left close to the same position, that is, somewhat bent, with the forearm hanging vertically from the elbow. The forearm is then in a position to aid in control by being moved slightly towards or away from the line of balance (b). If desired, the legs may now carefully be drawn together, although it is again a matter of personal preference and esthetic sense which position will finally be adopted.

Circus performers are frequently seen in very elastic poses while balancing, with the free arm and the legs in constant motion. This is permissible in show business, but it is considered poor form in gymnastics.

6a Free head balance

6. Free head balance*****

Perhaps ranking more as a circus type stunt than a gymnastic skill because it does necessitate the moving of arms and legs to maintain, the free head balance provides an impressive addition to a doubles balancing routine.

It is most easily learned from a straddle press, with the legs maintained almost parallel to the floor. Shift the weight almost entirely to the head while retaining fingertip ground contact with both hands (a), and then push off

6b

gently until the weight rests on the head (b). An invaluable aid for this stunt is
a padded ring or grommet four to six inches in diameter which gives the head
considerably more support. A word of caution: approach this one gradually to
permit the neck muscles time to build up strength, otherwise early sessions
will produce very stiff necks.

PRESS-UPS TO THE HAND BALANCE

Press-ups to the hand balance are similar to those used to enter the head
balance, but require considerably more strength since the arms alone support
the body weight.

7. **Bent arm tuck press*****

Squat down with the hands placed shoulder width apart so that the knees are just in line or in contact with the elbows. Bend the arms forward, the forearms remaining vertical, and raise the hips by pushing off with the toes (a). All the weight is now transferred to the arms, which should not be permitted to bend past the 90° angle (parallel to the floor). As the toes leave the mat, the legs are tightly tucked and rotated by the hips to a position above the body (b), where they are then extended. The body line approaches the line of balance gradually as the arms are straightened (c). As an additional challenge, once this stage has been mastered, start by sitting on the mat, legs extended, with the hands placed beside the hips. Lift off into an "L" support, then tuck and rotate the legs between the hands and on up to the balance.

Pointers: Pressing up requires more strength than the average beginner possesses, and bent arm moves are not generally performed by women, who rely more on flexibility to accomplish some of the straight arm presses to be described in following paragraphs. A few special techniques for the men will permit the necessary strength to be built up gradually, however. One method consists of pushing off quickly, or jumping with both feet to bring the hips and legs past the most strenuous level, or "sticking point," of the press-up. The arms will then not have to be bent as much, making extending them much easier. Also, straightening or whipping the legs upward forcefully provides momentum to aid in extending the arms.

One of the best methods to build strength in any exercise is to perform the move in reverse. Starting from the hand balance, bend the arms, and lower and rotate the legs in a tuck until they touch the floor. Numerous repetitions of this procedure over a period of time will strengthen the muscles involved to the point where it can be done in a slow, controlled fashion, and allow the action to be stopped at any point along the way. When this degree of control has been reached, the performer will find that going up will no longer present a problem.

As a complementary exercise to acquire strength for these moves, kick up against a wall with a moderate overbalance. Practice dipping or lowering the body repeatedly by bending the arms, gradually at first, over a period of time, until the nose touches the mat. Use a pillow if a mat is not available to avoid injury should the arms collapse. A spotting partner can be very helpful in all pressing moves by supporting the hips as required at the most critical times.

7a Hand balance bent arm tuck press

7b

7c

8a Hand balance bent arm straddle   **9a Hand balance bent arm pike**
    press   **press**

8. Bent arm straddle press****

As in pressing to the head stand, the legs are straddled, weight resting on the arms, and the hips are raised close to the line of balance (a). The cautions against permitting the arms to bend past the 90° angle are in effect here as in most bent arm presses.

Slide the toes forward until they lift off, and then rotate from the hips until fully extended. As a balance is reached, the arms are straightened, pushing the shoulders upwards and back to the line directly over the hands, and the legs are drawn together. The closer the hips are brought to the final position at the beginning of the press, the easier it will be.

9. Bent arm pike press****

This press is executed using the same procedure as in the straddle, but the legs are kept together throughout (a).

10. Bent arm arched back, or hollow back, press*****

From the previous press-ups to the hollow-back is a large jump, but this advanced move is included here because it is performed with bent arms. Unlike the others, in fact, the arms may at times be bent well past the right angle, and the strength requirements are correspondingly greater.

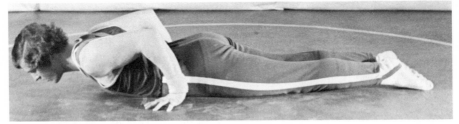

10a Hand balance bent arm arched back press

10b Hand balance bent arm arched back press

Begin by lying prone on the floor or between the ground bars. Place the hands at the sides near the hips (a). Arch the body strongly, and rock back and then forward onto the chest. Press vigorously with the arms to raise the body into a bent arm balance stance (b), and then press up, straightening the arms.

The technique for this move, also, may be best learned by going in reverse, i.e., starting with the hand balance, and lowering slowly to the prone position. The advanced balancer can execute the press without using any rolling momentum at the start.

11a Hand balance straight arm tuck press

11b

11. Straight arm tuck press****

What the straight arm press-ups eliminate in need of arm-straightening power, they more than make up for in shoulder and upper back strength requisites. Rotating the entire body by use of shoulders alone may prove to be a very discouraging prospect, but persistent attempts will gradually develop the necessary muscles. Improving flexibility of the lower back and the backs of the legs through stretching exercises will do much to reduce the leverage loads imposed during these moves.

Assume the same starting posture as in the bent arm tuck press, but keep the arms straight. Raise the hips as high as possible by extending the legs, keeping the thighs close to the chest and leaning the arms well forward (a). The balance is quite awkward at this point, and the balancer may find that there is a tendency to fall forward. It is this forward lean, however, which permits the weight shift needed to reach a balancing point. As the toes lift off the ground, tuck tightly and rotate the legs around and up (b). The shoulders are pulled back to the balance line in synchronization with the changing leverage loads imposed by the position of the legs.

Here too, use the reverse technique as a learning aid. The move should also be practiced starting from an "L" support on the floor. A spotter can assist the straight arm presses by standing at the head side of the balancer and supporting the hips as required during the crucial phases.

12a Hand balance straight arm straddle press

12. Straight arm straddle press*****

Straddle the legs moderately, bend sharply from the hips, and place the hands on the floor or bars quite close to the foot line, arms straight (a). Lean forward, rise on toes to place the hips high and, if needed in the beginning, hop off slightly to start the motion. The most difficult phase of this press occurs just as the toes leave the ground, at the point of maximum leverage. The back must not be permitted to drop as the legs rise, or the rotation will become more difficult.

**13a Hand balance straight arm
   pike press**

13. Straight arm pike press*****

The hands are placed on either side of the feet, contrary to the straddle press; the rest of the procedure being the same (a). Variations in body structure will permit some balancers to assume the initial position more easily than others.

14. Straight arm straight body press*****

Probably considered the most difficult of all the press-ups, this one has only been mastered by a relative handful of athletes. Beginning in a push-up position, the entire straight body is rotated about the shoulders and into the hand balance. It can be done, but no one need hang his head in shame if it is found to be beyond his capabilities. The planche, described in (**18**), must first be attained.

15. Press to a one arm balance*****

Another of the moves to be accomplished by the esoteric few only. Place one hand on the ground or bar as if performing a slow motion cartwheel. Lean strongly to the side, stretching the free arm well out for leverage, and raise the upper leg as high as possible while pushing off from the supporting leg (a). Lower the free arm as the balance is reached (b).

As with a number of leverage moves, a certain body structure may be needed to make this feat possible.

15a Press to a one arm hand balance

15b

LEVERS

16a Two arm lever

16. Two arm lever**

Kneel down and place the hands on the floor with the fingers pointing back towards the knees, or grasp one ground bar in an underhand grip. Lower the body until the hips rest on the elbows, lean forward and straighten the legs. The body should be straight or moderately arched, and parallel with the floor (a). The arms may have to be extended past a right angle to permit the legs to lift off.

17. One arm lever***

It is a bit easier to use the bars for this stunt, as the free hand can assist by applying leverage. Kneel down at about a 45° angle to the right bar and grasp it with an underhand grip. Grasp the other bar with the left hand, and have someone stand on the cross pieces to hold it down during the first attempts. Place the right elbow well into the hip, rather more towards the center of the abdomen, and slide the legs out straight into a straddle. The upper body should be maintained horizontal as the legs are lifted.

The beginner usually tries to lift the legs by pulling down with the free arm

17a One arm lever

17b

and lowering the body so that the face almost touches the floor. This approach must be corrected as soon as the performer has had some measure of success with raising the legs. The proper way to shift the weight is by straightening the right arm past the right angle while remaining horizontal. The toes aid in establishing the balance, and as they are lifted slowly, the legs are drawn together (a). As experience is gained, remove the left hand from the bar and extend it ahead in line with the body (b). This is an intriguing and impressive balance which is not too difficult to master.

The lever should be perfected on both sides, and the performer can shift from one side to the other by passing through the bent arm balance position. On the ground, this side-to-side shifting may be extended into an "alligator walk" by moving each free hand a few inches forward between each shift.

PLANCHES

18a Planche

18. Planche*****

Begin with a hand balance, and lower the straight body towards the horizontal while sharply leaning the shoulders forward (a). The arms are to be kept straight throughout. This balance requires great strength of back and shoulders.

19a One arm planche

19. One arm planche*****

Starting from a one arm balance with feet together, lower slowly to the side until approximately horizontal. The body is usually very strongly arched at this point (a).

Exceptional performers have been known to hold this balance in a frontal position, i.e., with the front of the body facing the floor rather than turned to the side.

PART II

Doubles Balancing

WORKING TOGETHER

It takes a certain amount of time and practice for balancing partners to acquire confidence in one another, as well as the skills to learn individual moves. The bottom balancer, or understander (referred to as B in the following text), is generally somewhat heavier and stronger than the top balancer (T). It is an excellent idea, however, occasionally to exchange places in order for both to have a greater appreciation of the difficulties involved in each balancer's role in the team. One of the greatest psychological lessons to be learned is that progress will be much faster if the bottom balancer is permitted to do the actual controlling, while the top mounter rigidly maintains a pose. This is often not an easy adjustment to make, and much time and effort can be wasted if both partners are unwittingly fighting each other for control. Both must maintain concentration and have a thorough understanding of all aspects of the attempted maneuvers. Spotters, also, should be carefully briefed, although advanced partners may wish to practice most of their routines without assistance.

It is suggested that the skills described here be practiced often, and that smoothness and full control be the goal at each step along the way, not only for the satisfaction to be gained from a job well done, but for safety's sake as well.

Some of the exercises detailed are best performed by male teams due to strength requirements, while others are suited to mixed or female teams. The methods shown for entering into the various holds and balances are not necessarily the ones used when performing combinations and routines, but are offered as a means of practicing them individually.

Grip note: The proper grip for most hand to hand work consists of a hand shake type, with the special additional technique of separating the fore and middle fingers so that they lie on either side of the partner's wrist. This may feel somewhat uncomfortable at first, but provides a "locking" action resulting in a more positive grip.

BALANCES AND POSES

20a Chest balance

20. Chest balance*

B assumes a kneeling position on all fours, the back horizontal. T stands to one side, places the chest on B's back, and slides arms under B's chest, grasping firmly. T then kicks up as in the head balance, bringing feet together (a). The pose may be varied with a straddle or stag.

21a Knee and shoulder balance

21. Knee and shoulder balance*

B is in a supine position with knees well drawn up and feet flat on the floor, separated about 12 inches. T steps in between B's legs, places hands on B's lower thighs and rests shoulders on B's upraised hands. Both partners must have their arms extended (a). The position is a bit awkward for T, and beginners usually attempt to bend the arms and support most of their own weight as in a bent arm balance. This only turns a simple balance into a strenuous one. Let B support the entire weight of T, T's arms only being used for leverage and control. T then performs a single leg kick-up or a tuck press. The latter is more easily controlled as it can be done slowly. The balance should be momentarily halted with T in a tuck, hips overhead (b). At this point both B and T should check for straight arms, with a comfortable support. T may then slowly extend the legs to the final pose (c), using the center of B's chest as visual reference. B ought to have T's feet in sight for best balance control.

The knee and shoulder balance provides an excellent opportunity for balancers to acquire a feel and awareness of body position and weight distribution. After the initial erratic attempts, beginners are invariably

21b

amazed at the ease with which this balance can be performed when properly done.

Variations, such as straddle and pike pressing (d), and repeated lowering and raising legs in these configurations are strongly recommended for additional skill development.

21c

21d

22a Ankle toss

22. Ankle toss*

T assumes a position similar to performing a back extension, with B grasping T's ankles (a). T momentarily lowers legs and then vigorously extends, pushing off with the hands as B lifts and pushes T's legs away to aid in the rotation (b). T lands on feet facing B (c).

22b

22c

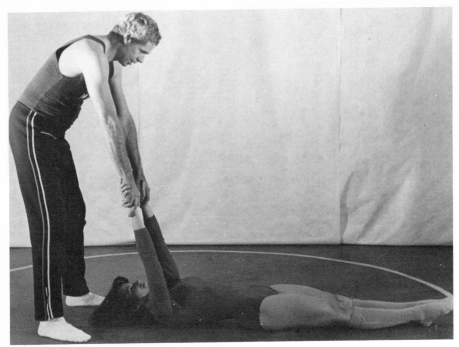

23a Cannonball

23b

23c

23. Cannonball*

B stands a short distance from the head of supine T, grasping T's hands (a). T quickly rolls into a tight tuck, which B can help hold by placing thumbs on the soles of T's feet. Almost simultaneously, B lifts and swings T first between the legs (b), and then forward. The forward swing must be accompanied by a strong lifting and straightening from B's shoulders and back, as T snaps into a layout (c). Both release their grips, and T travels through a graceful arch to land upright. B releases the thumb hold a split second before disengaging hands, allowing T to extend and obtain maximum lifting action. Properly executed, T should land firmly, with little or no extra forward momentum, and of course should not lose balance backwards.

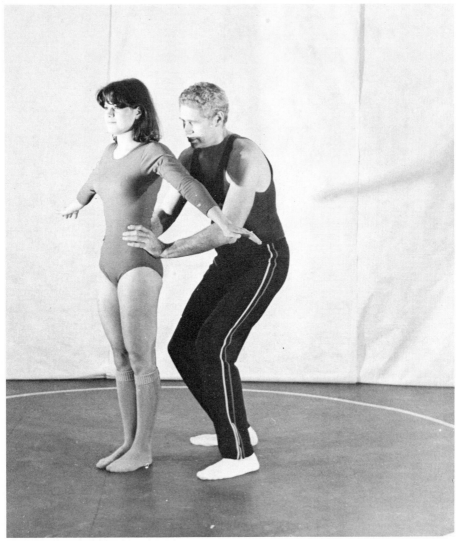

24a Side saddle sit on shoulder

24. Side saddle sit on shoulder*

In (a), B stands behind T, placing hands on T's waist. T rises on toes, both quickly lower to a moderate crouch, then drive upwards, B lifting with the arms to increase the momentum derived from the leg extensions. B then places T on one shoulder in the side saddle position (b). Note that T maintains stability by contacting B with the extended leg. B also gives support with the head and right arm. After a balance is secured, B may extend the arm (c).

24b

24c

25a Hold-out facing out

25. Hold-out

*Facing out**

Standing close behind, B grasps T's waist, and T grasps B's wrists for support (a). T lowers and recoils upwards as B lifts and places T on thighs (b). As T lands, B lowers into a semi-sitting position to absorb the force, then shifts hands to T's thighs, and slowly leans back, extending the arms. B must allow T to lean forward enough to counterbalance. T stands in an arched pose with arms outstretched (c).

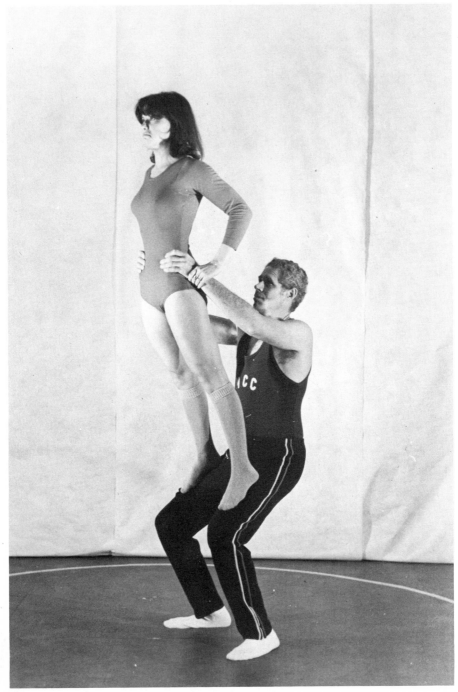

25b

25c

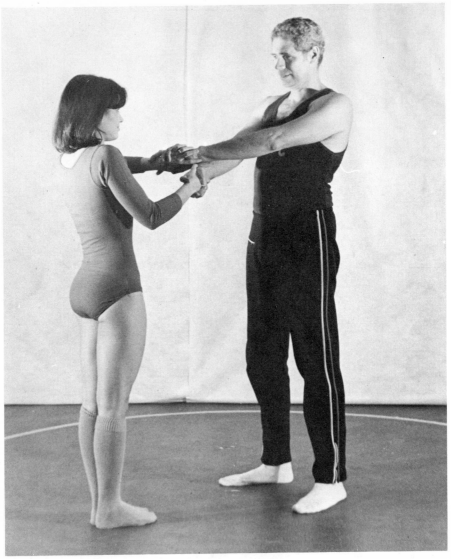

25d Hold-out facing in

*Facing in**

Facing one another, the partners join hands in a cross grip, i.e., right hand to right hand and left to left (d). B semi-squats and T steps onto B's thighs, one at a time. This move must be done smoothly, keeping tension with arms bent, and T must impose the weight gradually on B or B will easily lose balance. Both then carefully lean backwards, straightening the arms (e). When both of

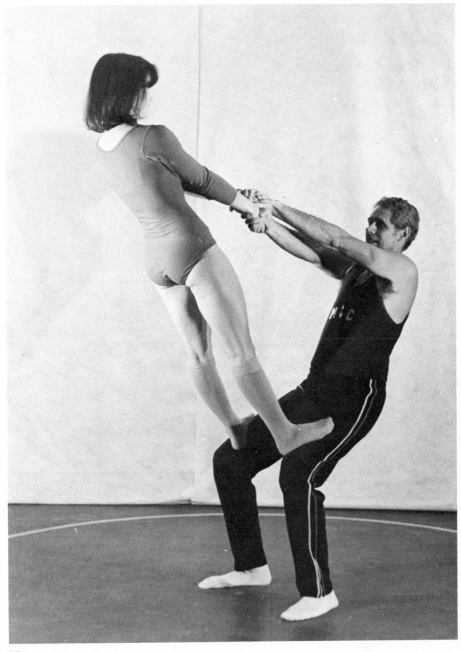

25e

their arms are extended, they may release their grip on either right or left
hands and assume the position shown in (f).

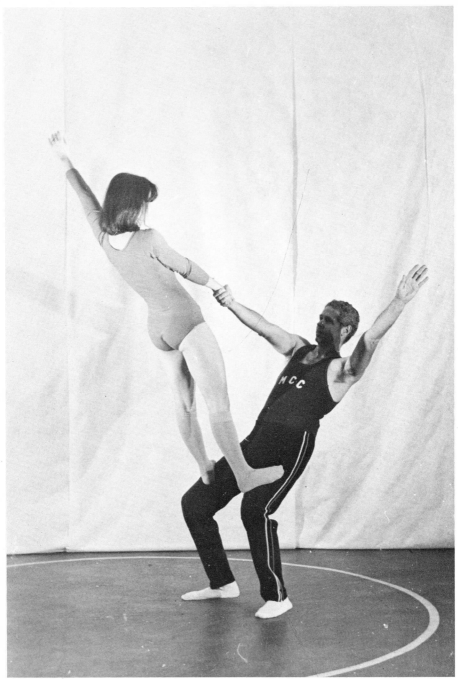

25f

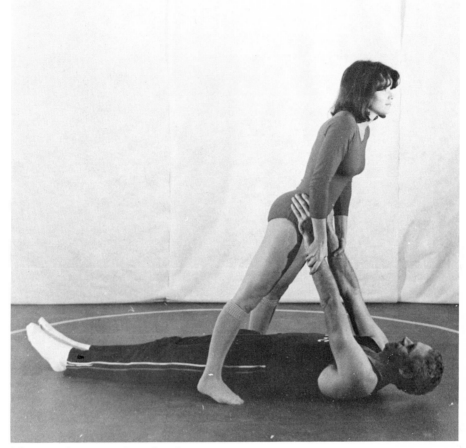

26a Low front angel on hands

26. Angel

*Low front on hands**

T straddles supine B, who places hands on T's hip bones, while T grasps B's wrists (a). T then leans forward, resting the entire weight on B's arms, which should be approaching the perpendicular at this time. T lifts legs to the horizontal, arches back (b), and extends arms to the sides as the balance is reached (c). Since each performer's body structure will vary, B will have to experiment with the exact hand placement in order to find T's balance point. B maintains the balance through wrist action, but T can initially assist by moving the arms forward or backward to determine the best position.

26b

26c

26d Low front angel on feet

*Low front on feet**

B is supine with legs bent and raised to the proper height to rest on T's hip bones (d). Partners grasp hands and pull as T jumps upward and forward. When the balance position is reached, they release hands, and T extends arms to the sides (e).

26e

Although the feet provide an easier support for T, there is a tendency on B's part to allow the hips to roll to either side, losing the balance. B's hips must remain in contact with the mat as much as possible. In addition, B may use the hands to stabilize the legs once T has released the grip.

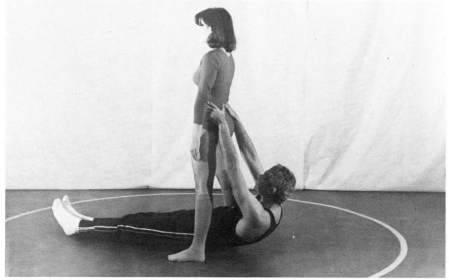

26f Low back angel on hands

26g

Low back on hands*

This move is somewhat awkward to enter into, but is easier to learn in this position, although it may be used to greater advantage in the high stance.

T straddles B, facing away. B reaches up and places hands on T's hips (f). T then arches back, stretching the arms overhead, and brings one leg up into a stag pose (g). It is necessary to raise one leg in order to shift the weight sufficiently, since B's hands are not at the correct point to balance T with both legs extended.

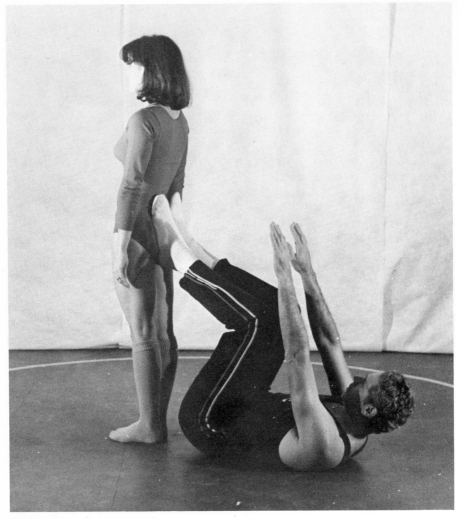

26h Low back angel on feet

*Low back on feet**

B places feet on T's buttocks, with the toes supporting the small of the back (h). T performs a back bend, grasping B's upraised hands, then pushes off firmly with the legs as B pulls with the arms and extends the legs to the vertical (i). The partners release hands and both extend them to the sides or overhead. T should not sag limply, but assume a rigid but graceful arch (j).

26i

26j

26k High front angel

*High front***

Standing facing each other, B places hands on T's hip bones, and T places hands on B's shoulders (k). T crouches and springs upward, also pressing down firmly with the hands. B almost simultaneously drives erect with forceful leg extensions and pushes the arms overhead (l). The thrust must be continuous, with no hesitation. T assists the lift with the arm pressure on B's shoulders until B's arms are "locked" out, then releases and extends the arms sideways as the legs rise and the body arches (m). Proper speed, timing and coordination will do much to relieve the strength requirements for B.

Should T overbalance strongly, the best recovery is simply to go limp as B steps back and lowers T to a shoulder.

261

26m

26n High back angel

High back**

Standing facing the same direction as T, B places hands on T's hips (n). T then rises on toes, crouches and springs strongly upward and backward as B also drives erect and pushes T overhead. T extends arms overhead, and draws one leg into a stag pose as the final position is approached (o).

This move requires more strength on B's part, as T cannot assist in weight support, although the action of throwing the arms overhead vigorously aids considerably. Here again, T strives to direct the line of the jump in close to B so that B can exert the most efficient ''pressing'' action.

260

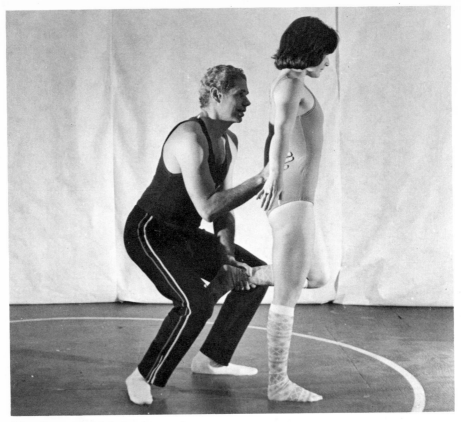

26p One arm high back angel

One arm high back**

B crouches behind and somewhat to the side of T, grasping T's ankle and placing the right hand at the base of T's spine (p). This hand position is very critical to the balance, and care must be taken to locate the same spot consistently, and not to permit the hand to lose contact or shift during the leap. T then lowers and rapidly propels upwards by strongly extending both legs, at the same time throwing the arms upwards and over (q). Unless T places considerable weight on the left leg, B will not be able to use the left arm to assist in the lift, and may not have sufficient strength to "press" T aloft with the right arm alone. T must also direct the leap backwards in order to keep the c.g. directly over B. If T is properly balanced, B may release the grip on the left ankle and extend arm (r).

To dismount, B can regrasp T's ankle, lower T to one shoulder, and thence to the ground.

26q

26r

27a Stand on shoulders

27. Stand on shoulders*

After joining hands in a cross grip (a), B semi-squats, while T places the right foot on B's right thigh (b). B raises the left arm overhead. T then steps up, using downward arm pressure to assist, rotates, and places the left foot on B's left shoulder (c). It is important to keep close-in while stepping up, much as in the correct technique of mounting a horse, in order to minimize the effort

27b

and the unbalancing forces. T stands erect using shin pressure against B's
head for stability as B shifts grip to T's calves (d). After confidence has been
gained, B may extend arms to the sides (e).

Although not a difficult move, a number of repetitions of this stand will be
required before T feels comfortable. With a tall bottom balancer especially, T
finds the floor a long way down. To aid in building confidence, partners may
prefer to practice with B kneeling on one leg.

27c

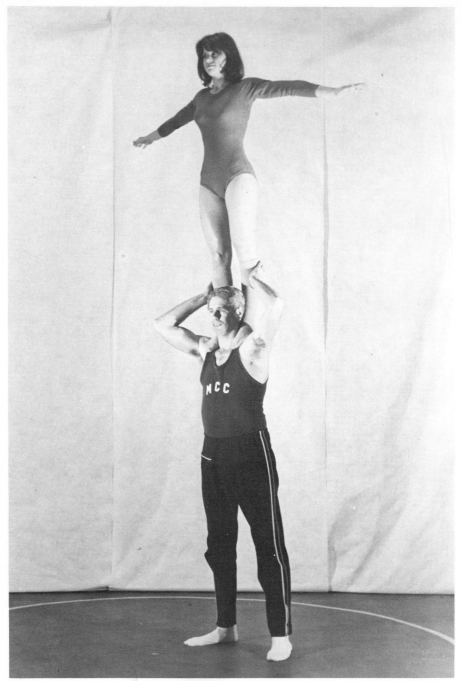

27d

27e

To dismount, T may gently leap forward, with B catching at the waist to ease the ground impact. Another method is to again join hands, T sliding legs down while using arms for support, to finish sitting on B's shoulders (f). B then squats and places T's feet on the floor.

27f

28. Half lever, or "L"

This pose is generally used as a momentary preliminary to, or recovery from, another move, as holding it for any length of time requires considerable abdominal strength.

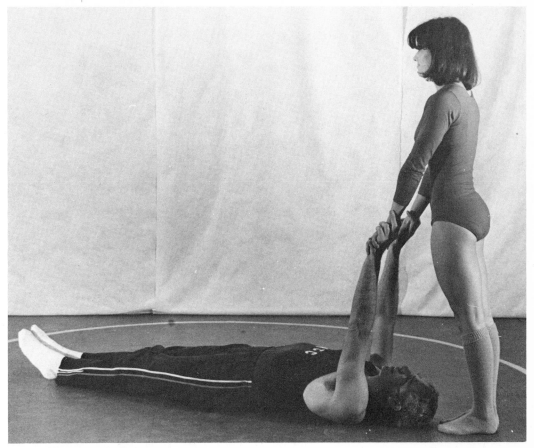

28a Low half lever

*Low**

The first attempts at a free hand to hand support will probably be quite shaky, but practice will gradually bring greater stability. T may enter by standing at B's head and grasping B's upraised hands (a). T's weight is then transferred to B's arms, and then T smoothly lifts and swings the legs through to the lever (b).

In swinging through, T should avoid sudden jerky movements that might result in B's losing control of the support. It may be helpful to provide additional support for both partners in the beginning by pressing the hands in close to T's sides.

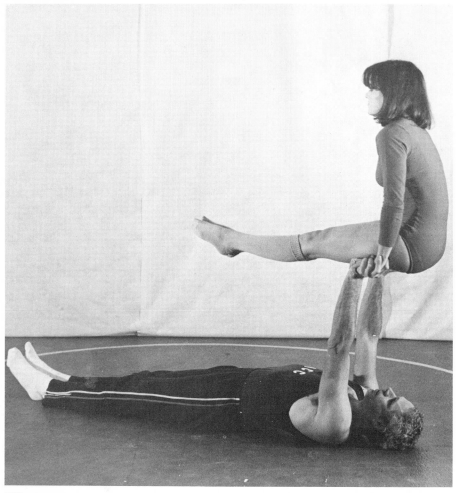

28b

28c High half lever

High**

Partner's grasp hands in ''lock grip'' behind T's back (c). To aid in timing the coordinated jump, B counts aloud (one, two, . . .) while swinging the gripped hands outward through a small arc, and back in again. On the prearranged swing, both crouch, and T recoils strongly as B drives erect (d). T's movement somewhat precedes that of B, giving time for T to straighten the arms. If T's arms bend during the lift, B will have no solid resistance to push against, and may fail to drive T overhead. A word of caution to T at this point: avoid kicking heels into B's abdominal region!

As in the low position, B can assure additional support by keeping the hands pressed in close to T's sides. As soon as B's arms are locked overhead, T draws the legs into the ''L'' (e). As proficiency is gained, the entire move will proceed smoothly without intermediate stops.

To dismount, B lowers the arms and crouches as T lowers the legs to contact the floor (f).

28d

28e

28f

29. Straddle support

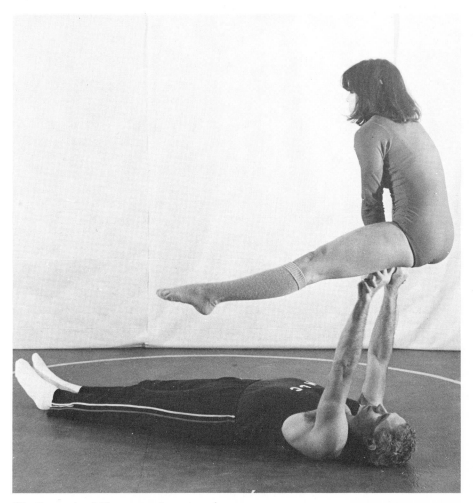

29a Low straddle support

*Low**

   T stands at the head of supine B, grasps B's upraised hands and smoothly transfers the weight while lifting the hips and raising the legs to a straddle (a).

29b High straddle support

High**

T enters the straddle from a stand on B's shoulders (b,c). As in all overhead supports, B must keep the arms directly overhead and increase the support

29c

base by placing one foot somewhat behind the other. T can dismount by returning the feet to the stand on B's shoulders, followed by the techniques described in (**27**).

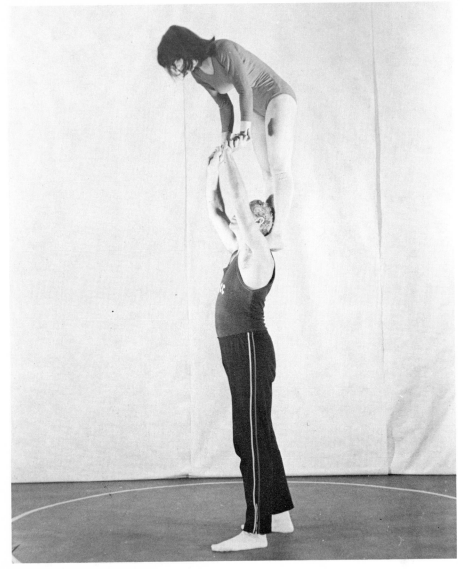

30a Front somersault dismount from stand on shoulders

30. Front somersault dismount

Although not difficult moves, somersault dismounts from a height are initially frightening, and should be well spotted. They may be done slowly at first, but will actually be much easier once the confidence to perform them briskly has been gained.

30b

From stand on shoulders*

B should provide a rigid arm support to assist T in rotating as high as possible. T bends at the waist, bringing the shoulders down to a bent arm support position (a), and springs off B's shoulders while ducking the head to

30c

aid in the rotation (b). At the same time B bends slightly at the knees and rebounds, giving T additional momentum. B gives arm support throughout the somersault and assists T in landing smoothly (c).

30d Front somersault dismount from straddle support

*From straddle support***

Here also, B must supply a rigid support (d), and endeavor to keep the arms as high as possible in order to permit T to complete the rotation and land in an upright stance. In a continuous, smooth movement, T ducks the head, bends

30e

the arms, and rotates the hips over and around (e), straightening from the waist when the upper body is again upright. The landing shock, of course, is absorbed by bending the knees upon ground contact, which is made on the balls of the feet rather than on the heels.

31a Pitch back

31. Pitch back***

B stands in a crouched position with hands locked and wrists or forearms resting on thighs (a). The hands will give best support if the following grip is used: the left hand is held open, palm up and thumb extended. Reach under with the right hand, also palm up, and grasp the left thumb so that the right fingers curl over onto the mouse of the left hand. Elbows should be held in close to the sides.

T approaches with a brisk walk (not a run!), places both hands on B's shoulders, and steps onto B's tightly gripped hands (b). As T steps straight up with a strong leg extension, B rises from the crouch and lifts the hands as high as strength permits. The rotation is accomplished mainly by T's throwing the head back and then tucking quickly, but is aided by B following through until the lifting hands lose contact (c). T rotates in the tuck and extends to touch the mat in a good impact absorbing stance, landing once again facing B (d).

It is important to use two spotters and a strong belt while learning this stunt. A number of straight-up practice jumps should be made, without actually performing the back somersault, to gain familiarity with the initial stages. The most common fault of the beginner is not to step up on B's hands, but permit

31b

31c

the leg to be pushed in the bent position. It is practically impossible to gain sufficient height unless the take-off leg is fully extended. Each spotter grasps one side of T's belt (in an undergrip that will unwind as T rotates), and follows the approach. The spotters should be alert to over-rotation as well as under-rotation, but usually will not have to supply any lift if the take-off has been correctly performed.

31d

31e

As confidence is gained, one spotter only can be used, and then the spotting gradually reduced to a follow-through without contact.

The pitch back may also be performed with straight legs in a pike, or entirely extended in a full layout (e). The latter requires a more vigorous take-off to secure additional height, and a more positive rotational assist by B.

32a "V" seat

32. "V" seat

Partners enter into a low back angel on feet (a). T then first slowly places hands along thighs, and then carefully assumes a piked sitting position with the hands grasping the calves (b). The "V" seat can be practiced solo on the floor first. As T raises the back past the horizontal, the legs may be drawn up, bending at the knees, and the calves are then grasped. Slowly extend the legs

32b

to the "V" pose. The balance is a bit more precarious when seated on B's feet, and B must keep in full foot contact for best support.

Return to the angel with equally slow movements, lowering the hands to the sides close to the body, and extending them overhead once the arched angel stance has been resumed. If the arms are extended overhead prior to laying back into the angel, the descent may be rather abrupt due to the additional leverage load.

33a Hand to hand back walkover

33. Hand to hand back walkover*

In the back angel position, partners regrasp hands (a). B draws T's arms downward while pushing T's hips higher by rolling over further on the back, and T raises one leg in the direction of the walkover (b). B should plant the elbows firmly on the mat to give T solid support during the intermediate phase of the walkover, but can extend the arm as T's leading foot contacts the ground (c). The move may be performed quickly, or with a momentary halt as T passes through the balance point.

33b

33c

33d

33e

A variation which some partners may find preferable is for B to grasp T's upper arms instead of the hands during the walkover (d,e).

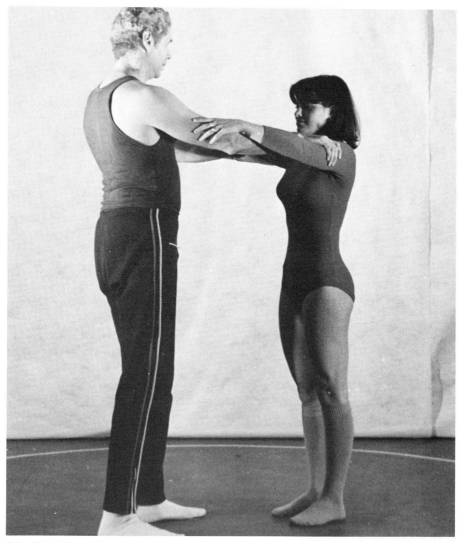

34a Foot flag

34. Foot flag**

Partners face each other and grasp arms (a) as described in **(39)**—Arm to arm balance. B semi-squats, T steps onto B's thighs, shifts the total weight to the left leg, and releases the right arm grip. T then raises the right leg, places the heel on B's left shoulder while hooking the foot behind B's neck. B grasps T's right calf with the free left hand, and releasing the other arm grip, grasps T's left calf, as T slowly lowers back into an arched pose (b). While lowering,

34b

34c

34d

T should maintain the arms close to the sides to reduce the leverage load. When approximately horizontal, T raises the arms overhead, and, depending on the stability of the pose, B may release the right calf (c). Advanced performers may have B release both hand supports.

Instead of reversing moves to recover, B regrasps, slowly lowers T into a back walkover, and pushes T's legs through the balance point into that maneuver (d).

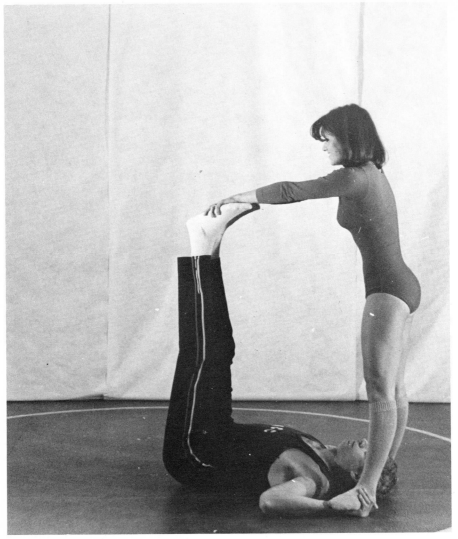

35a Low low hand to foot balance

35. Hand to foot balance

*Low low**

B assumes a supine position with legs raised. T steps on B's hands, one at a time, while holding B's feet for balance (a). During the first attempts, B may leave the legs in this position to assist T in gaining familiarity with the

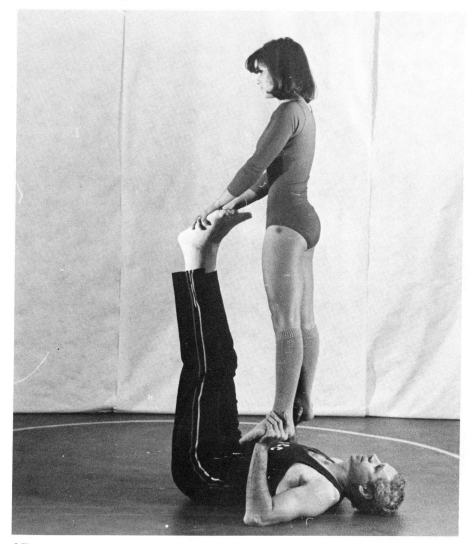

35b

maneuver. T then jumps upwards and forwards, supporting some of the bodyweight with the arms. As T rises, B presses strongly and rotates the arms to rest the elbows on the floor, forearms vertical (b). Next, T releases B's feet and carefully stands erect and rigid, arms extended sideways while B lowers legs to the mat (c). If T holds a rigid stance, B will be able to do the balancing with wrist action.

While learning this stunt, T may experience foot or calf cramps due to

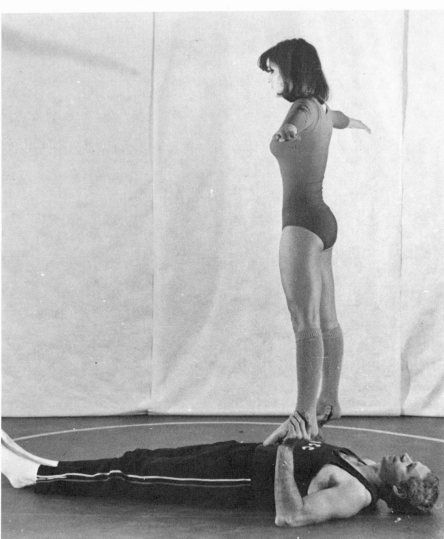

35c

overtension of muscles. This tendency can be avoided if B has a comfortable grip on T's feet. Also, as the partners become more proficient, they will find that the balance becomes quite steady, permitting them to hold the position without undue effort.

To lower, one method is simply to reverse the procedure. In another technique, T regrasps B's feet and swings the legs through while supporting the entire body weight with the arms. B's legs are carried forward, permitting

35d

T to land clear (d).

  After sufficient practice, T can jump to the low low position without the aid of B's legs. A spotter may assist by standing astride of B, facing T, and holding T's hands. T should attempt the move without depending on the spotter's support, and avoid bending forward at the waist. It is a natural tendency at first to bend forward to avoid falling backwards, and beginners find it disconcerting to have their feet restricted from moving freely.

35e Low hand to foot balance

*Low***

From the low low position (c), B presses T upwards, fully extending the arms (e). Note that T has been displaced laterally a short distance while being raised, and can assist B by leaning slightly backwards from the ankles until the lift has been completed. Return by lowering to the low low, leaning slightly forward from the ankles during the move, and dismounting as previously described.

Once the straight arm balance feels comfortable, or if B does not have sufficient strength to perform the lift, T may mount by leaping directly to the low position (e) from the starting point (a). Do so without the aid of B's legs, which should be extended.

The partners will find it useful to gain confidence by shifting weight from one foot to the other, and jiggling around in the balance as well as holding perfectly still.

35f Intermediate hand to foot balance

Intermediate***

Acquire some feeling of confidence in the stand on shoulders (**27**) before attempting this balance, as T's head will be quite high above the mat, and considerable courage will be required to stand on a relatively unstable base.

T shifts the weight to one leg and raises the other sufficiently to permit B to slip the hand under and grasp T's foot. B can offer calf support with the free hand during this phase (f). Next T shifts the weight to the foot being held by B, lifting the other to permit B to grasp it (g). Practice shifting back and forth from shoulders to hands until this operation can be performed smoothly and without panic.

35g

*High*****

From intermediate (g), B must press T aloft unaided, maintaining balance through wrist action, until the arms are fully extended. T can only assist by maintaining a rigid pose throughout (h).

If balance is lost at any time during the lift, B must rapidly lower T, then

35h High hand to foot balance

release and grasp T around the waist to soften the ground impact.

Normal dismount procedure involves lowering T to shoulder level and shifting back to the stand on shoulders as described, then descending to the ground as suggested in (**27**).

35i One hand to foot balance

*One hand to foot****

When partners are able to maintain a very stable pose, they may attempt shifting to a one hand support. T draws the legs together and shifts the weight to one side. B releases the grip on the unburdened foot and uses the free hand to steady the supporting arm. A front scale or an arabesque is an attractive stance in this balance, and it may be performed low low, low (i), intermediate, or high. To dismount, reverse the procedure.

With an exceptionally stable balance, B may release the steadying hand and extend it to the side.

36a Toss to high hand to foot balance

36. Toss to high hand to foot****

B assumes a lunge position (a), placing one forearm along the thigh, palm up. T steps onto B's hand and also grasps B's other, upraised hand. T forcefully extends the mounting leg and drives rapidly upwards, assisted by a downward pull on the grasped hand and the momentum gained by vigorously raising the free arm. As T reaches full thrust, B begins to lift and drive erect (b).

36b

As B's lifting hand approaches shoulder level, the supporting wrist must rotate outward, so that T turns to face the same direction as B, passing the unsupported leg in front of B's face. B releases the upstretched hand and quickly grasps T's other foot (c). From here, B presses T to the final overhead position (d).

36c

With practice, it is possible to gain sufficient momentum to drive past mid position (c), decreasing the force required by B during the latter part of the lift. As a preparatory exercise, B may lower into a kneeling position to have T acquire a feel for the initial phases of the toss at a lower level. However, since

36d

B cannot use the legs for lifting in this method, it does place much more of a load on the arms.

Hint to B: try this with a lighter partner first.

37a Elbow roll

37. Elbow roll***

Begin with a low hand to foot balance (a). B draws the left knee up, the foot remaining on the mat, while lowering the right elbow to a point near the head (b). T maintains an equal distribution of weight on both legs during this phase, but then shifts slightly and momentarily to the right leg to help B turn to the prone position while lowering the left arm parallel to the right one (c). B's forearms must be kept vertical or the balance will be difficult to hold, especially while moving.

B now draws the right knee up to gain leverage to initiate the completing turn, and T momentarily unweights the right leg to allow B to raise that arm while turning (d). When B is again supine, T steps up on the right leg as B extends the left arm (e).

This stunt is best done with four distinct stops, as some of the intervening positions are awkward to hold. A spotter can be used to hold T's hands while walking T through the maneuver. Much of the move's success depends on T's ability to shift weight at the correct time.

37b

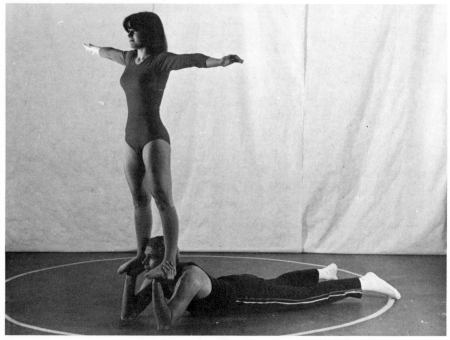

37c

37d

37e

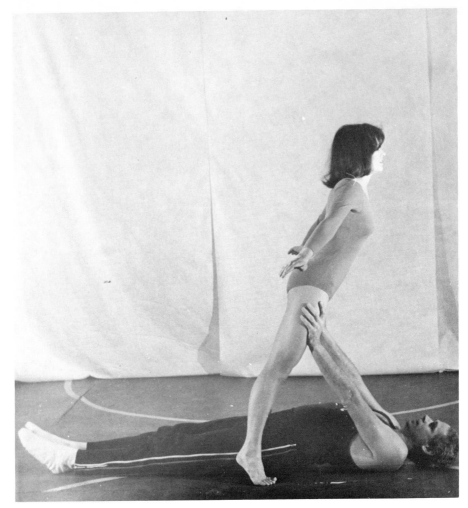

38a Low thigh balance

38. Thigh balance

*Low**

   T straddles the supine B, who grasps T's upper thighs (a). T leans forward
from the ankles and extends the arms to the sides and somewhat to the rear. B
pushes T off the ground into the balance, and T draws the legs together (b).

38b

Notice that T is standing erect with a well arched back. Unless the center of gravity is brought to a point behind T, the immediate tendency is for T to topple forward as soon as the feet leave the floor. The pose shown is actually a very stable one, and B should not find it necessary to grasp T's thighs tightly at all.

38c High thigh balance

*High***

B must crouch fairly low to get into the starting position (c). At the signal, T lowers and recoils rapidly upwards, throwing the arms for additional momentum. Although T jumps slightly forward to get directly over B, care must be taken not to bend forward at the waist, but maintain the erect posture described above.

B drives erect at the same time to increase T's thrust, and presses T overhead (d). Some difficulty may be experienced in completely "locking

38d

out'' the arms due to the closeness of the grip, and B should strive to support T well overhead to reduce the strain.

When lowering, B should support T until ground contact is made.

39a Low arm to arm balance

39. Arm to arm balance

*Low**

As shown (a), B's arms must be straight, with the hands gripping T's upper arms at the junction with the shoulders. T's arms lie outside of B's, and grasp the backs of B's upper arms just above the elbows. There will, of course, be some variation in T's gripping point depending on the relative lengths of each partner's arms, but B should fix the grip first, with T adjusting as necessary.

B's shoulders must be firmly planted to provide a stable support. T jumps

39b

with both legs to place the hips on the balance line, and tucks in tightly (b).
After a momentary pause to establish balance, T slowly and carefully extends
the legs to the final position (c). If T grasps firmly and assumes a rigid stance,
B should have no difficulty in controlling the balance. In case of an overbalance, B can twist T off in a prearranged direction to permit T to land feet
first.

Beginners usually find themselves moving and swaying quite a bit, but

39c

practice will soon eliminate this superfluous motion. Another common error is for T to exert too much lateral pressure on B's arms when jumping, which either causes B to overcompensate wildly as T's feet leave the ground, or immediately forces B's arms past the recovery point.

The balance should also be worked using the straddle procedure instead of the tuck. As described in knee and shoulder balance (**21**), it is an excellent idea to practice raising and lowering the legs without touching the ground.

39d High arm to arm balance

High * * *

Using the same grip described in the low balance, partners stand facing each other. B will find that stationing one foot somewhat ahead of the other will offer a much more stable base (d).

39e

Coordinating the initial jump is aided by a slight up and down "pumping" action of the arms, together with a verbal count. On the agreed-upon signal, T springs into a straddle around B's chest, high under B's arms (e). B bends at

39f

the waist, lowering T's head close to the mat (f), and immediately recoils, swinging the arms overhead. T maintains the straddle, using it as a lever to raise the hips as high as B's swinging action permits, then releases the leg grip

39g

to hold a momentary balance in a tucked (g) or a straddle. If this position feels secure, T extends to the final balance (h).

The most common problem in learning this move is in T releasing the leg

39h

grip too early. When this is permitted to occur, B is called upon to swing the entire weight of T aloft by use of the arms alone, a difficult task with all but very small top balancers. Another tendency to avoid in arm to arm balancing

39i

is for T to sag down so that the partners' heads are almost touching. To avoid this, T should try to stretch high by straightening the arms as much as possible. Also, T may at first experience a "sticking point" where the hips are not quite high enough to permit the press-up to be completed. T may find it helpful to push off with the toes from B's chest. Should an overbalance occur, B simply turns around, changing the direction of T's fall to an underbalanced condition, and maintains support until T's feet touch the floor.

In a controlled dismount, T should balance down through a tuck or

39j

straddle, and not just fall with extended body. Another method of lowering consists of exactly reversing the mounting procedure.

A more spectacular technique of lowering is that of the roll-down. B lowers T until their heads are almost touching, then both tuck their heads under, B bends forward and T pikes sharply, and executes a forward roll down B's back (i). There should be a brief pause in position to be certain that T will not slip off before releasing the arms. T walks out, one leg at a time, to make a smoother ground contact (j).

39k Back extension to low arm to arm balance

39l

*Back extension to low arm to arm balance****

As illustrated (k), partners lie head to head using the arm to arm grasp. B exerts a strain to resist T's pull as T rapidly pikes (l) and forcefully snaps into an extension. As T develops momentum, B pulls strongly and rotates the arms into the low position (m).

39m

Since there is some lateral movement involved, T must direct the extension somewhat towards a line vertically through B's shoulders instead of directly overhead as in a solo extension into a head or hand balance.

40a Shoulder balance on feet

40. Shoulder balance on feet**

B is supine with arms and legs raised. T stands at B's head, grasps B's hands, places shoulders on B's feet (a), and hops or presses into a tuck before extending (b). When the balance is stable, T shifts grip to B's legs, one arm at

40b

a time (c). The most difficult part of this balance is in maintaining the stability in B's leg position. The hips must be firmly planted, and B can use the hands to aid in leg support once T has released them.

40c

The balance may also be done in the opposite direction, but mounting then becomes a problem. B must first bend the legs, resting the thighs on the chest, then extend once T has reached the balance.

41a Two arm hand balance on thighs   41b

41. Hand balance on thighs

*Two arm***

T places both hands on B's thighs just above the knees, and B grasps T at the waist as shown (a). As T executes a kick-up, B supplies as much lifting action as may be required to place T into a hand balance. At this point B's arms are still bent, and B is fairly upright. Carefully counterbalancing, B leans backward while straightening the arms (b).

It is helpful for a spotter to stand behind B during the early attempts, in case of a backwards loss of balance.

41c One arm hand balance on thigh

One arm***

Instead of leaning back and straightening the arms, B remains close to the balanced T, who proceeds to straddle and shift the weight to one arm (c). With practice, B should be able to both support and balance T enough to release one hand (d). Really advanced top balancers are able to hold this position unsup-

41d

ported, but even with a one handed assist the stunt is quite impressive.

A useful method of dismounting is for T to return to the two arm balance, then lower to a bent arm balance. From here, with B exerting full support, T hops both hands to the mat, extending the arms, and then performs a forward roll or walkover as B releases.

42a Hand balance on knees

42. Hand balance on knees**

B assumes a sitting position, knees drawn up, supporting T's upper arms as

42b

T grasps B's knees (a). T kicks up into a hand balance, bending the arms to enable the hips and legs to travel the additional height of the base. B can assist T in straightening the arms if necessary (b).

43a Hand balance on arms

43b

43. Hand balance on arms***

T stands behind B, who is seated with arms crossed over knees, head ducked, and grasps B's upper arms (a). Either a very strong kick-up, or else a jump to a tuck press may be used to enter the balance position (b). B can only assist by supplying a rigid and stable base.

44a Hand balance on forearm

44. Hand balance on forearm***

This balance is best entered from the one arm high back angel (**26r**).
After the angel pose has stabilized, B carefully rotates T about 90°, and

44b

raises the left arm to permit T to grasp it (a). B then lowers the arm to the side, with the forearm extending at right angles to the body, thereby drawing T down as in a back walkover (b). B's wrists must also tip downward to permit T to follow this movement. In order to shift the weight to a proper balance, T extends the raised leg to assume a split stance. When balanced, B withdraws

44c

the back-supporting arm and extends it to the side (c). The balance is not completely free, as T has the right arm pressed against B's side. B can aid the balance by leaning in the appropriate direction. T should grasp B's forearm quite close to the elbow with the right hand to reduce the leverage on B. An impressive, yet not too difficult additional refinement of this balance is

44d

possible if T is able to raise the left arm and perform a one arm balance (d).

Various methods of recovery are available from this balance. One may be effected by reversing the procedure, to return to the one arm back angel. Another is simply for T to lower as though completing a back walkover (approaching the ground chest down), but landing with both feet together.

44e

A third method is shown (e), where B has replaced the back support and lowers T as through a front walkover. Here B must fully support T until the first leg makes ground contact, and follow through with the left arm to be certain T has completed the move.

45a Low butterfly

45b

45. Butterfly

Low*

Although this stunt is generally performed in the high position, it is easier to learn low first.

Begin in a low front angel on hands (a). T grasps B's right arm near the shoulder and supports part of the body weight, permitting B to shift the right

45c

45d

hand somewhat more to T's side. T also lowers the left leg as shown (b). Maintaining the right leg quite high, T now rotates over onto B's right hand. B assists by raising the left shoulder and pushing off with the left hand and fingers.

With the balance established, B extends the left arm, using the right wrist alone for control (c), and then T releases the grip on B's shoulder (d). The key to this balance lies in finding the exact balance point on T's hip for B's supporting hand.

45e High butterfly

High***

From a high front angel (e), the same technique as in the low pose is used.

45f

As T rotates, B lowers the right shoulder while stretching the left to assist by
pushing off with the left fingers (f,g). As before, with a very stable balance, T

45g

may also extend the other arm (h), with B maintaining control through wrist action only.

45h

46. Hand to hand balance

It will be helpful for partners to review the material covered in the hand to foot moves (**35**).

46a Low low hand to hand balance

Low low**

With B supine, elbows on the ground and forearms vertical, T grasps B's hands in the lock grip, standing with the stemming leg to one side of B's head (a).

The kick-up must be quite vigorous because of the additional height, and T should lean well forward. To recover from a severe overbalance, B assists T in twisting off in a pre-arranged direction. It will be very helpful for T to go through a number of intentional overbalances in order to acquire confidence in kicking up. Once in a balance (b), the most important point to work on is for T to maintain a rigid pose, and for the partners to grip hands firmly to allow B to control the balance by wrist action.

46b

The position of the wrists will vary with different partners according to comfort, from a very high (with hands almost in a line with the forearms) to a very low (with hands close to right angles with the forearms). Very naturally there will be considerable shaking at the beginning, but this condition will improve with practice. A spotter can be of assistance by straddling B and catching T's legs as they approach the balance.

Practice variations in the balance, such as straddle and stag poses, for further control experience.

**46c Low hand to hand
balance**

46d

Low***

Unless B presses T from the low low to this position (f), it will be necessary for T to perform a press-up. Since there is no rigid base for T to work from, pressing up is fairly difficult. The bent arm, tucked method is the easiest to

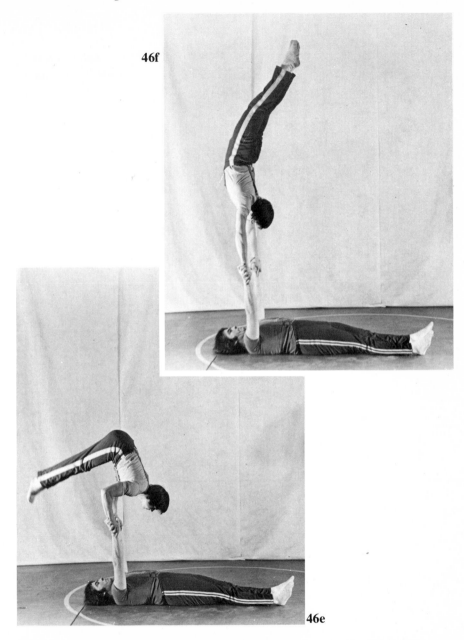

46f

46e

begin with, and then any of the others described in the singles balancing section may be worked up to. For example, beginning with a half lever in the low position (c), T curls the hips through in a bent arm tuck (d), or a pike press (e).

**46g Front angel on feet
with toss to low hand to
hand balance**

46h

*Front angel on feet with toss*****

From position shown (g), with crossed grip, B bends the legs slightly and T
lowers the legs to a pike position. T then whips the legs upwards into an arch
as B vigorously extends the legs, tossing and rotating T into the balance (h,i).

46i

**46j Back extension to low
        hand to hand balance**

46k

Back extension****

T assumes a supine position on the already supine B, with partners
grasping hands (j). The exact position must be determined by individual
experiment, but once established must be carefully noted. B has legs separated to give T a stable starting base. T then pikes and rolls backward rapidly
(k) as described in the back extension to the head balance (**1**) and the hand
balance (**4**). As T snaps into the hand balance, B must have the elbows firmly

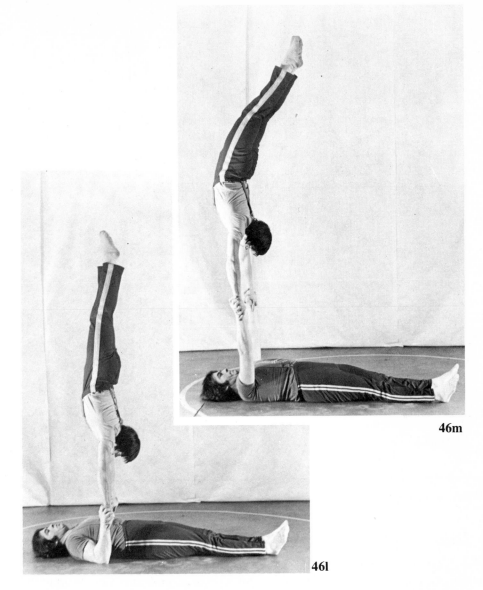

46m

46l

planted in the low low position to give T a solid foundation to push against (l). B then immediately presses T into the low position (m). The entire sequence must be performed in a continuous motion in order to develop sufficient momentum to put T at arms length without intermediate hesitations.

The starting position may also be entered by T standing at B's head, grasping hands as if preparing to press into a balance, but then, as B lowers the arms, ducking and rolling over slowly until supine (j).

46n Intermediate hand to hand balance   **46o**

*Intermediate*****

As preparation for learning the high balance, the bent arm position (for B) may be entered from the stand on shoulders (n). T performs a press-up to the balance (o). The basic techniques and recovery are as described in the following paragraphs on the high position.

*High******

The easiest method of getting into this balance is from the stand on shoulders (p). From here, T performs a tuck press into the balance (q).

B should have one leg slightly advanced for a more stable base, and keep

46p High hand to hand balance **46q**

the arms in a good line with the body for best skeletal support. In case of an overbalance, T twists off, and B must follow through with support until T makes ground contact. Intentional overbalance recoveries should be practiced in order to help T overcome shyness in pressing up at this height. Lack of confidence in recovering from an overbalance is probably responsible for most of the problems in performing properly balanced press-ups. There is a great tendency to remain underbalanced during these mounts, which really makes them much more strenuous than they should be.

Another method of entering the balance is to jump to a support, as described in the high half lever (**28**). Once overhead, T can perform any of the standard press-up techniques.

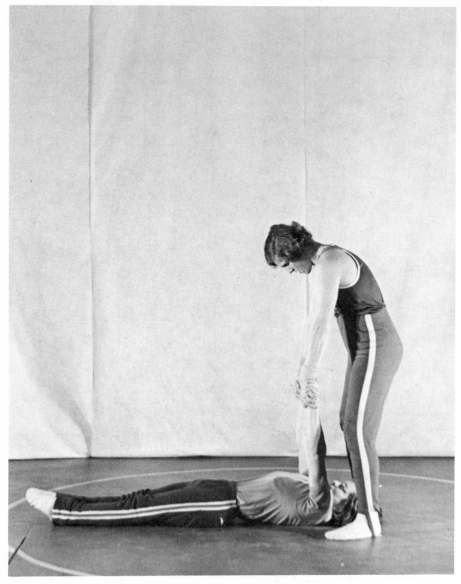

46r Straddle extension to high hand to hand balance

*Straddle extension******

This is a more elaborate mount, and requires somewhat more strength on B's part.

From the supine position (r), T extends smoothly, straddling under B's

46s **46t**

armpits (s). B straightens and leans back, pulling T into a momentary seat on
B's chest. There should be sufficient lift to permit B to tuck the elbows under
and hold T in a bent arm support (t). B then presses T overhead in a smooth,
continuous motion (u), whereupon T can press up to the balance (v).

46u   **46v**

When performed correctly, enough momentum can be gained in this mount to reduce much of the work load on B's arms in lifting T overhead.

47. Balance levers

Both the two arm and the one arm levers may be worked in either a modified form, with arm support, or strictly free as when performed solo. Review the discussions of both of the free balances.

47a Modified low two arm lever

47b

Modified low two arm*

T straddles the supine B, using an undergrasp to hold B's forearms just above the elbows. B supports T's bent arms at the biceps (a). T leans well forward and raises the legs parallel to the ground (b).

47c Modified high two arm lever

*Modified high two arm***

Partners stand facing one another and grasp arms (c) as described in the previous paragraph (low position). On the signal, T leaps upward and forward

47d   **47e**

as B lifts and extends arms well overhead (d). T then assumes the lever position (e).

This position may also be entered by lowering from a high arm to arm, although the grip is not quite proper.

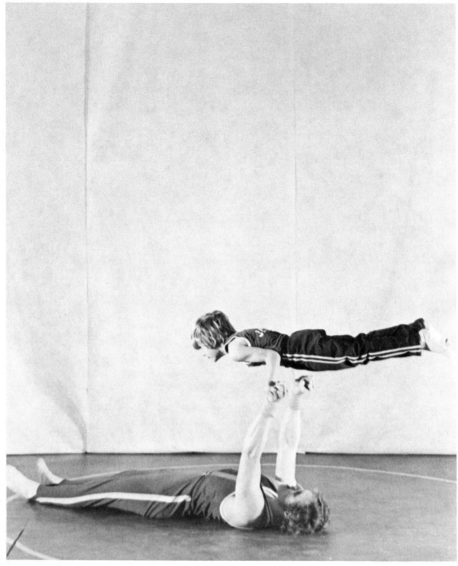

47f Free low two arm lever

*Free low two arm****

The alignment of the wrists presents some difficulty (f) since a reverse grip is easier for T but awkward for B. The problem may be solved by clasping hands instead of using the lock grip, but it is more difficult to enter the balance this way from any preceding pose.

47g Free high two arm lever

*Free high two arm*****

As in the low position, clasping hands is the only practical method of holding the balance, which may be entered from the stand on shoulders. The awkwardness of the hand grip and wrist alignment (g) really make it impractical for anything but an isolated demonstration.

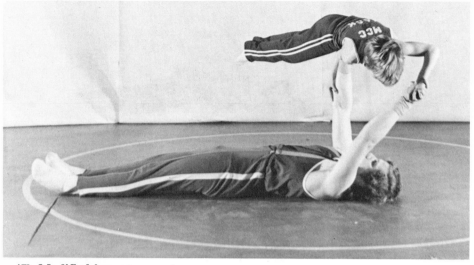

47h Modified low one arm lever

47i

*Modified low one arm***

  T stands to one side of supine B, and partners use the grasp described in the modified two arm lever, except of course, on one arm only. The other hands are clasped to aid T in assuming the horizontal position (h). When the balance is secure, the assisting hands are released (i).

47j Modified high one arm lever

47k

*Modified high one arm*****

As this balance is difficult to enter into from a stand on shoulders, it can be performed as part of routine in which B moves from a supine to a standing

47l   **47m**

position while supporting T in the lever (j, k, l, m). This move requires a considerable amount of strength on B's part, especially with a heavier partner, and of endurance on the part of T. Note that B rolls slightly to the left in order to place the left arm in a good supporting position (j, k).

47n Free low low one arm lever

47o Free low one arm lever

*Free low low and low one arm****

The prime requisites for these and the high positions are strength on the part
of B, and a very steady arm lever for T. They are best entered by lowering
from a hand to hand balance, as when performed solo.

It is advisable to practice the low low position first, since it permits B to
hold a steadier base by pressing the forearm to the side of the chest (n). B must
be careful to have the supporting shoulder firmly to the mat in the low position
(o).

47p Free intermediate one arm lever

47q Free high one arm lever

Free intermediate and high one arm*****

Here, too, it will be useful to practice in the intermediate support, i.e., with B's arm bent and pressed to the side (p).

As in the low positions, T enters by lowering from a hand to hand balance. B must stretch the single supporting arm high and press the shoulder against the head for extra rigidity (q).

48a Back lever

48b

48. Strength levers

Back**

T rests shoulders on B's thighs, and B grasps T's backwardly raised arms at the wrists (a). T then raises the legs slowly and smoothly in line with the body (b) as B leans back and supports T's weight by pulling with the arms.

Abrupt movements must be avoided as they will cause loss of balance for B. The closer to the vertical T is, the less strenuous this lever is to hold, but it looks best with T in a more inclined position.

48c Front lever

48d

Front***

B is in a shoulder bridge with arms in the low low hand to hand position. T grasps B's hands and places shoulders on B's thighs, head ducked under (c). T rotates from the shoulders in a pike to approximately the angle shown (d), then slowly straightens the body while continuing to lower to the horizontal. T's arms are bent at right angles, pulling B, who has by now straightened the arms, into the final position (e).

There is a tendency for T to slip upward on B's thighs which must be

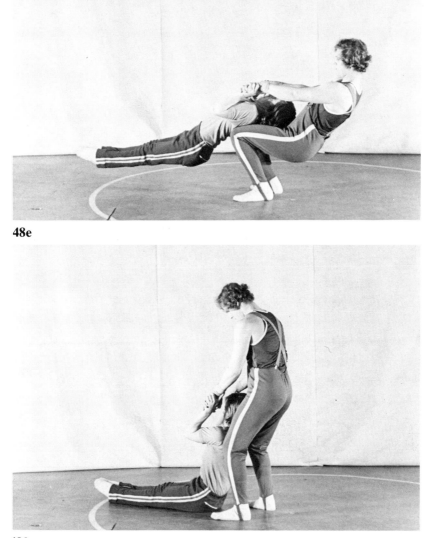

48e

48f

overcome by both partners keeping the arms quite rigid. Also, the pressure on T's shoulders may be painful if the position is not properly adjusted. At any rate, it should be mentioned that, although the balance itself is not too difficult, the stunt is quite strenuous and not a very comfortable one for T.

Another method of entering the lever is with T sitting on the ground in front of the standing B (f). B leans back, pulling T off the ground. T then extends as B reaches the final position, which may be more horizontal than illustrated here (e).

49a Double planche

49. Double planche***

The greatest strain in performing this balance is on B's neck, which will support much of T's weight. B starts out as if doing a push-up, and T rests chest down on B's upper back, clasping arms tightly around B's chest. The exact relative locations depend on the physical proportions of the partners, and will have to be determined by trial. T attempts exactly to counterbalance B, so that as T's feet lift off, B's legs will also be lifted, assisted by a slight leaning forward (a).

Both bodies, of course, must be held rigidly straight, and B must maintain the balance by wrist action.

Additional Very Difficult Possibilities

There are any number of other poses or balances which imaginative partners may attempt, but which may be beyond the capabilities of all but the strongest and most skillful.

The following are a few suggestions.

50a Low low free head balance

50. Free head balances****

Performed on one of B's hands in either low low (a), low (b), intermediate (c), or high positions (d).

May also be done head to head, with use of a grommet (e, f).

50b Low free head balance

50c Intermediate free head balance

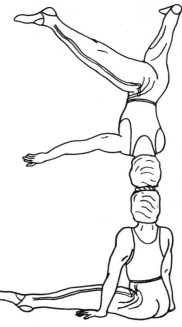

50e Intermediate head to head balance

50d High free head balance

50f High head to head balance

51a Flag

51. Flag***

52a Low low hand to hand planche

52b Low hand to hand planche

52. Hand to hand planches

Low low (a), low (b), intermediate (c), and high (d).

52c Intermediate hand to hand planche

52d High hand to hand planche

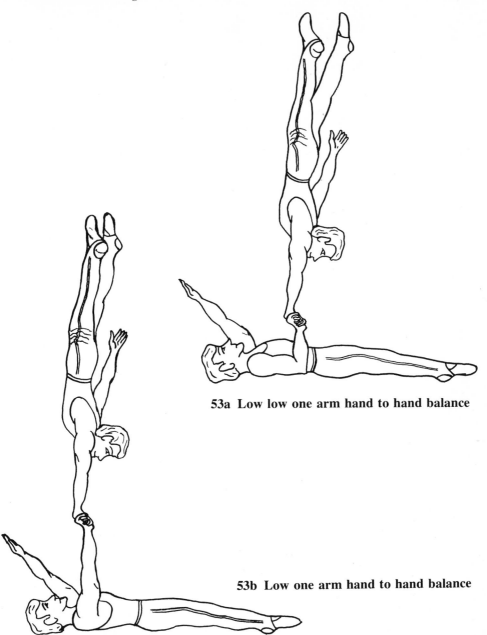

53a Low low one arm hand to hand balance

53b Low one arm hand to hand balance

53. One arm hand to hand balances*****

Low low (a), low (b), intermediate (c), and high (d). Variations of the hand to hand category here might also include: on B's thigh (e), and on B's head (f).

53c Intermediate one arm hand to hand balance

53d High one arm hand to hand balance

53e One arm hand to thigh balance

53f One arm hand to head balance

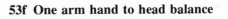

PART III

Combinations and Routines

OBJECTIVE

The ultimate objective of sport acrobatics is the smooth blending of individual stunts into an impressive and esthetic routine. Often, two or three moves or balances seem to offer themselves naturally to a short sequence or combination, groups of which may be arranged into longer routines. These combinations allow routines to be put together and altered or rearranged more easily for greater variety.

Many of the moves described in the previous text are actually brief combinations because they are entered from an already established pose or balance. Refer to the illustrations and texts mentioned in following examples.

EXAMPLES OF COMBINATIONS

54. From a **Hold-out facing in (25 d–f)**, partners regrasp hands. T shifts weight and right foot onto B's right thigh, thence mounts to a **Stand on shoulders (27 c–e)**.

55. Beginning with the **Back angel on feet (26 h–j)**, T performs a "V" seat **(32 a, b)**, then concludes with a **Hand to hand back walkover (33 a–e)**.

56. In the **Side saddle sit on shoulder (24 a–c)**, B lowers to a kneeling position (one leg) and T places the extended foot on B's horizontal thigh. T then does either a **Scale (XVIII)** or a **Frontal balance (XIX)**. B may support T in this pose if necessary.

57. T mounts to a **Stand on shoulders (27 a–e)**, then performs either a **Scale (XVIII)** or a **Frontal balance (XIX)**. B may use both hands to steady T's supporting leg. After returning the raised leg to B's shoulder, T uses a **Front somersault dismount (30a–c)**.

58. From a **Stand on shoulders (27 a–e),** both partners lean forward as one body until a fairly acute angle with the ground is reached. T then hops off B's shoulders, lands on feet, and both simultaneously dive into a **Forward roll (II, III).**

59. Starting with a **High front angel (26 k–m),** B crouches and bends arms slightly, then recoils immediately to toss and rotate T into a **High back angel (26 o).** T assists the rotation by throwing the left arm across the chest. B must be sure to drive directly upwards, as the tendency is to lose the balance in a forward direction.

60. Starting from a **Hold-out facing in (25 d–f),** partners regrasp both hands, and T turns around on B's thighs to a **Hold-out facing out (25 b, c),** then enters a **Side saddle sit on shoulder (24 b, c).**

61. In a **Low low hand to foot (35 c),** B raises legs between T's, and T sits on B's feet, lowering into a **Low back angel on feet (26 j).** T then does a **Hand to hand back walkover (33 a–e).**

62. From a **Low front angel on feet (26 e),** partners change directly to a **Low arm to arm balance (39 c),** B pushing T into that balance using the supporting legs.

63. Holding a **Knee and shoulder balance (21 c),** T shifts one arm at a time over to a **Low arm to arm balance (39 c).** B must initially grasp T's shoulders somewhat lower than normal in the knee and shoulder position.

64. Partners perform an **Elbow roll (37 a–e),** but do this in a **Low hand to hand balance (46 e)** instead of the low hand to foot. Although the basic procedure is the same, the maneuver is much more difficult.

65. T lowers from a **Low hand to hand balance (46 e)** to a **half lever (46 c),** then places the feet on B's drawn-up knees. Shooting forward in a tuck, T pulls B into a standing position, from whence the partners perform a **Hold-out facing out (25 c).**

66. Using either a **Low hand to foot balance (35 e),** or a **Low hand to hand balance (46 e),** B partially lowers T by bending the arms as T leans forward, permitting B to sit up. B then tucks one leg under, rises to the knees and thence to a standing position. T is now in an intermediate balance (either **35 g** or **46 o).** B then presses T overhead to the high position (either **35 h** or **46 g).** This combination requires a great deal of strength on B's part, as well as endurance for T in the hand balance.

EXAMPLES OF ROUTINES

Routines are an expression of individual tastes as well as skills. A great deal of variety is possible, and putting together a pleasing routine is a challenge to the imagination. The following routines are offered only as an indication of what can be done using only a few of the skills described in this book. Partners or solo performers can greatly extend their repertoires if they have further backgrounds in tumbling and dancing. Music, of course, can enhance any performance greatly, and no restrictions need be placed on the type used—popular or classical, orchestral or vocal.

Solo

67. An unusual balancing act may be put together using the **One arm lever (17)** and the **Hand balance (4).**

Construct a set of six to eight wooden blocks which measure 6 to 8 inches on a side, depending on what is most comfortable to your own grip. The blocks are placed in two stacks, about shoulder width apart. There are many variations, but the act generally uses the following format:

Enter the hand balance a short distance from the blocks, and walk over to them. Lower to a one arm lever, pick one block from the top of one stack, and place it on the floor. Shift to a lever on top of this block, and pick the top block from the next stack, placing it on the floor a comfortable distance away. Shift over to a lever on this block, and repeat the process, placing one block on top of the other, until all blocks are again stacked in two piles with you on top. Then press up to a hand balance. The advanced performer then executes a one arm balance, returns to the two arm balance, lowers to a bent arm position, and, shifting hands one at a time to the floor, walks away from the blocks. (At this point only the hardiest manage not to collapse from fatigue.)

Mixed or female team

68. High arm to arm (39 d–h), reverse steps to lower T to floor, step to a **Hold-out facing in (25 d–f),** directly mount to a **Stand on shoulders (27 c–e),** roll out as in combination **(58).** B stays supine on mat as T goes into a **Low hand to foot balance (35 e).** B then lowers T to a **Low low hand to foot balance (35 c),** and T swings through **(35 d)** to land on the floor. From here, perform a **Low back angel on feet (26 h–j),** followed by a **Hand to hand back walkover (33 a–e),** then T swings through on B's hands to a **Hold-out facing out (25 c),** as described in the latter half of combination **(65).** Place T in a **Side saddle sit on shoulder (24 b, c)**, thence to a **Scale (XVIII)** on B's thigh as in combination **(56)**. T steps down to the side and enters into a **Hand balance on thighs (41 a–d)**, then lower and dismount as in **(41)**, ending on floor. Finish off with a **Cannonball (24 a–c)**.

Mixed team

69. One arm high back angel (26 p–r) to a **Hand balance on forearm (44 a–d)**. T turns, mounts to a **High front angel (26 k–m)**, thence to a **High butterfly (45 e–d)**. T returns to the angel pose and B then flips T over to a **High back angel (26 o)** as described in combination **(59)**. B lowers T to one shoulder, thence to the floor, kicks up to a **Hand balance (4)** and does a forward roll out, ending supine on mat. T mounts directly to a **Low hand to foot balance (35 e)**, partners perform an **Elbow roll (37 a–e)**, and T swings through B's legs **(35 d)** to land on mat. **Low back angel on feet (26 h–j)**, **"V" seat (32 a, b)**, **Hand to hand back walkover (33 a–e)**, followed by a **Low low hand to hand balance (46 a, b)**. T twists off to one side to dismount and then pulls B to a standing position. Enter a **Foot flag (34 a–d)**, regrasp arms for a **High arm to arm balance (39 d–j)**. After rolling down, B turns and holds T in a **Hold-out facing in (25 d–f)**, T mounts to a **Stand on shoulders (27 c–e)** and performs a **Frontal balance (XIX)**. Follow with a **High straddle support (29 b, c)** and end with a **Front somersault dismount (30 d, e)**.

PART IV

Triples Balancing

The same techniques previously described are used in performing the various poses shown in the following photographs. A great deal of variety is possible here as well as in solo and doubles work, but the methods used to enter into the various positions will require considerable ingenuity on the part of the performers, since written descriptions easily become confusing.

POSSIBILITIES

70

71

72

75

76

78

79

80

81

83

85. Although multiples of more than three are beyond the scope of this book, an example of a 4-man balancing pose is included to illustrate such further possibilities.

Index of Positions and Balances

(Numbers in parentheses indicate Figure numbers)

223